BALLAH MAKES SHAPES

By Augustus Y. Voahn

Illustrations by
Shabamukama Osbert

VILLAGE TALES PUBLISHING

Dedication

This work is dedicated to the loving memory of my brother, Lee Deazie Dorliae; who departed this world in April 2013. His enthusiasm for life, his motivational behavior in getting things done, and his accurate mathematical skills at solving problems were the inspirations for this book. Lee, this is for you.

Text copyright © 2017 Augustus Y. Voahn
Illustrations copyright © 2017 Village Tales Publishing

All rights reserved. No part of this publication may be reproduced, distributed or transmitted in any form or by any means, without prior written permission.

Village Tales Publishing
www.villagetalespublishing.com
www.villagetalespublishing.com/childrenbook
www.oass.villagetalespublishing.com

This is a work of fiction. Names, characters, places, and incidents are a product of the author's imagination. Any resemblance to actual people, living or dead, is completely coincidental.

eISBN 9781945408205
ISBN 9781945408199
LCCN 2017908157

Formatting and Cover design by OASS

Printed in the United States of America

Hello Friends,
My name is Ballah Sumo.
I am six years old.
I am in the first grade.

I live in the Soul Clinic Community.
Soul Clinic is a big
community in Monrovia.
There are many houses there.
Some of the houses are big,
and some are small.
There are also many children.

This is my house.
In my house, there are six persons.
They are my father, my mother, my bigger sister, Wokie, Paye, our uncle, our grandmother and I.

I have a dog named, Tracer.
My sister does not like Tracer.
She calls him "Greedy"
because he eats too much.
She sometimes kicks him.
That makes me angry with her.

This is my school.
It is called,
the Hawa Binta Elementary School.
My teacher's name is, Miss Jallah.
She teaches us mathematics.

In my class I have a friend.
Her name is, Siah Garlo.
Siah is also my neighbor.

One day Miss Jallah
brought a new lesson called, 'Shapes'.
She taught us
the different types of shapes.
It was fun.

When I went home, I decided to make those shapes.

I asked my mother for a pair of scissors.

I asked my father
for some poster sheets.

I went into my room
and locked the door.
I did not want my sister, Wokie,
or even Tracer, to find me.
While in the room,
I began cutting the paper into
many different shapes and sizes.
I spent the whole evening doing this.
See what I made.

This is a triangle, just as Miss Jallah said.

This one is called a rectangle.

This one is called a square.

And, this is a circle.

I was very happy with my shapes.
I ran to call my friend, Siah.
I wanted her to see my shapes.

When Siah came, she was happy too.
"Let's make them in different colors,"
she said.
"Good idea. They will be very beautiful
with colors," I said.
So I opened my book bag
and took out a stack of color papers.
We began to cut the shapes.

Now see how our shapes look in color.
The triangle we made blue.
Rectangle became red.
The square turned yellow,
and the circle was green.

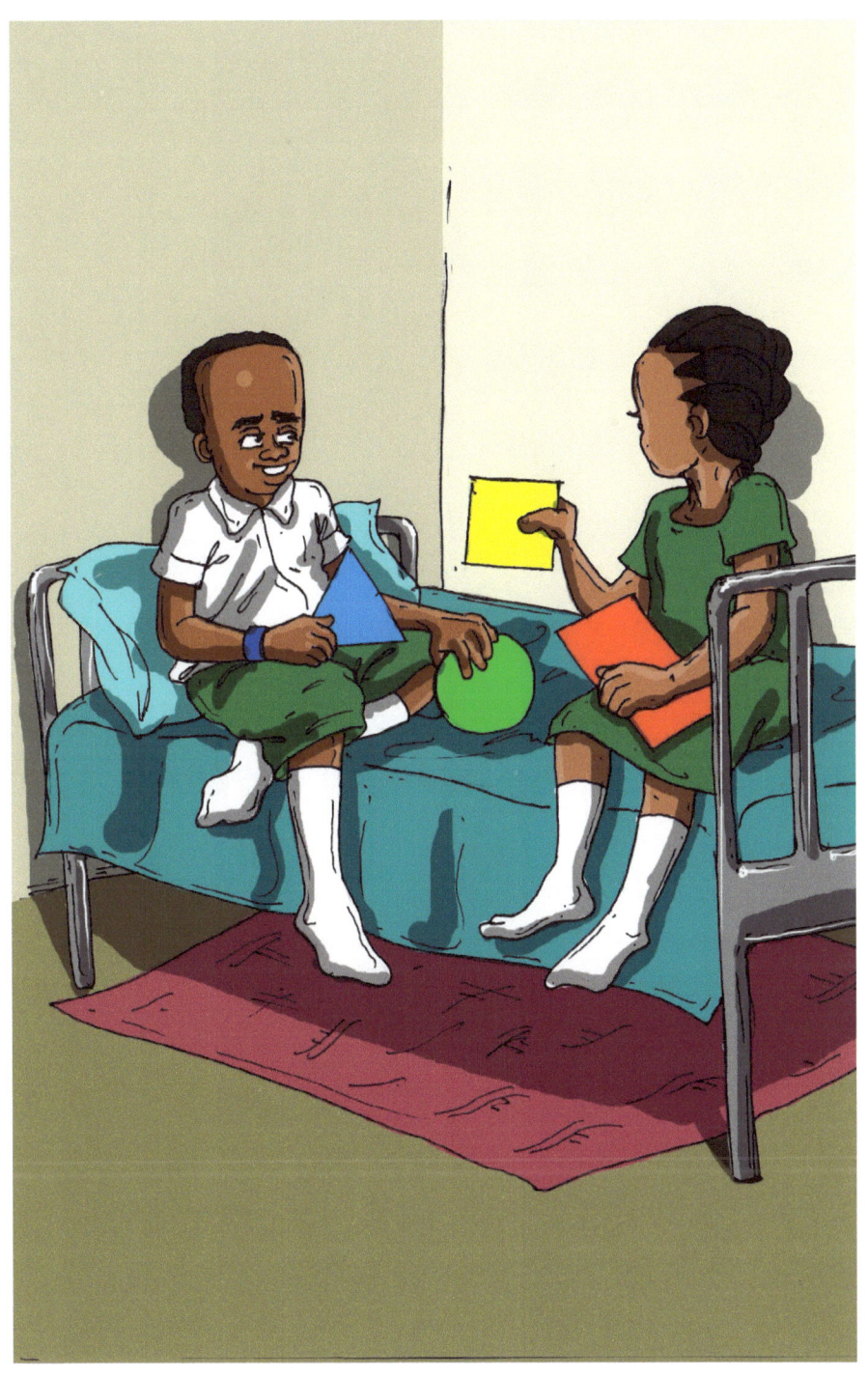

The next day
we took our shapes to school.
We showed them to Miss Jallah.
Miss Jallah liked our shapes.

"So you made them by yourselves?"
she asked.
We nodded our heads.
"Good students!" she said.
"You are very good students."

She told us to stand in front of the class with our shapes. Our friends clapped for us. We were so proud.

Miss Jallah said they were fine.
"Aren't these shapes beautiful,"
she asked the class.
"Yes!" they answered.
"Now, I want everyone
to make shapes like these and bring
them to class tomorrow," she said.
Siah and I were very happy.

The next day,
everyone in my class
had many different types and colors
of shapes. We were all happy.

More shapes to learn and make...
2D Shapes

Circle

Triangle
has 3 sides

Square
has 4 sides

Rectangle
has 4 sides

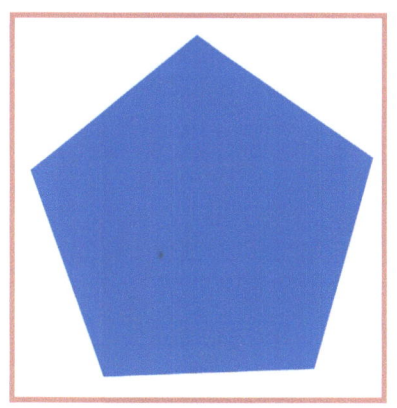

**Pentagon
has 5 sides**

**Hexagon
has 6 sides**

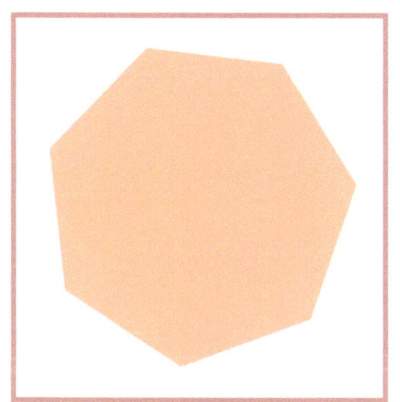

**Heptagon
has 7 sides**

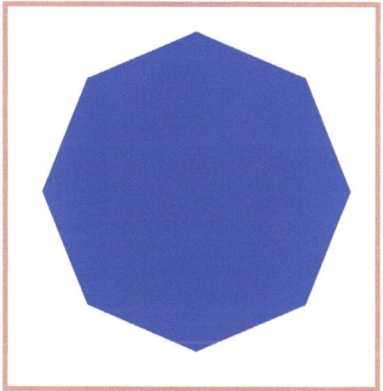

**Octagon
has 8 sides**

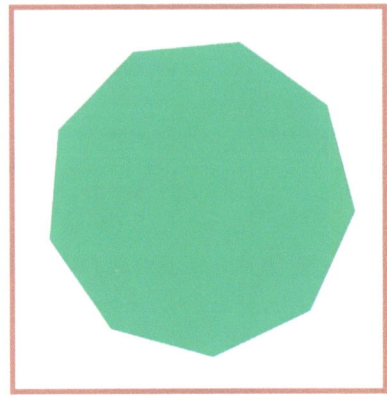

Nonagon has 9 sides

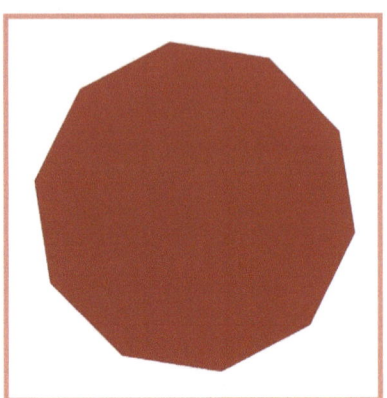

Decagon has 10 sides

Star

Heart

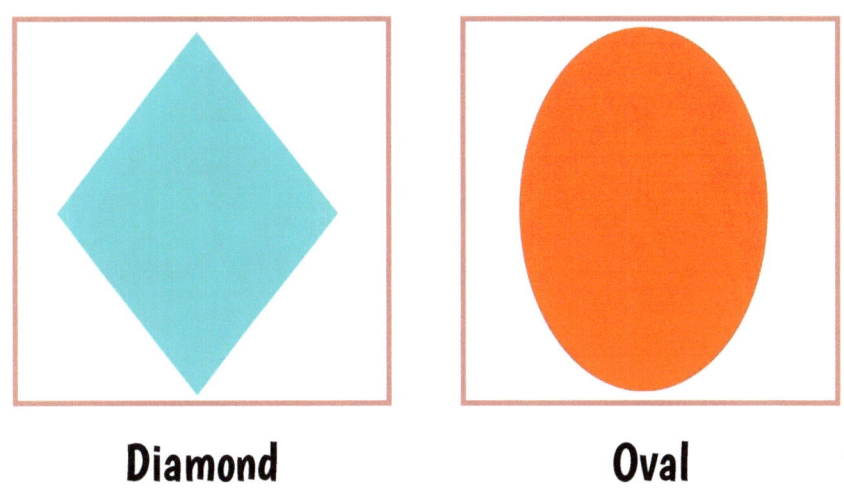

Diamond **Oval**

Below are some 3D Shapes

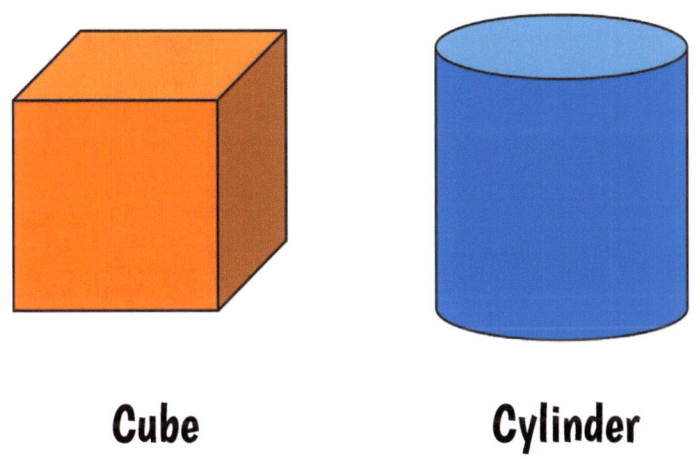

Cube **Cylinder**

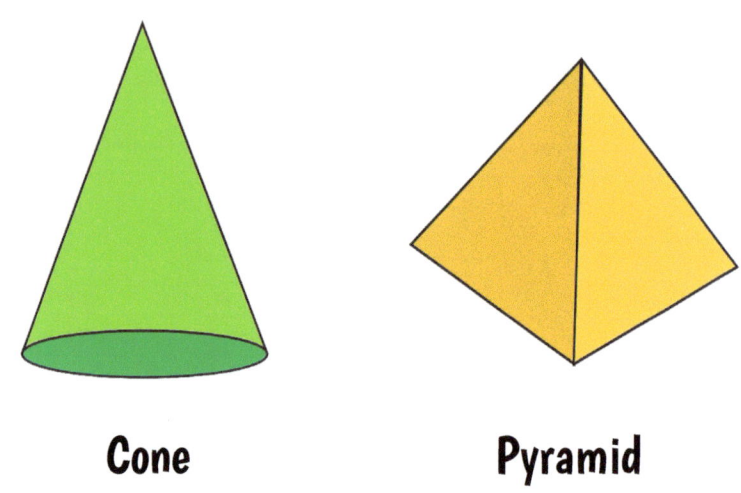

Cone **Pyramid**

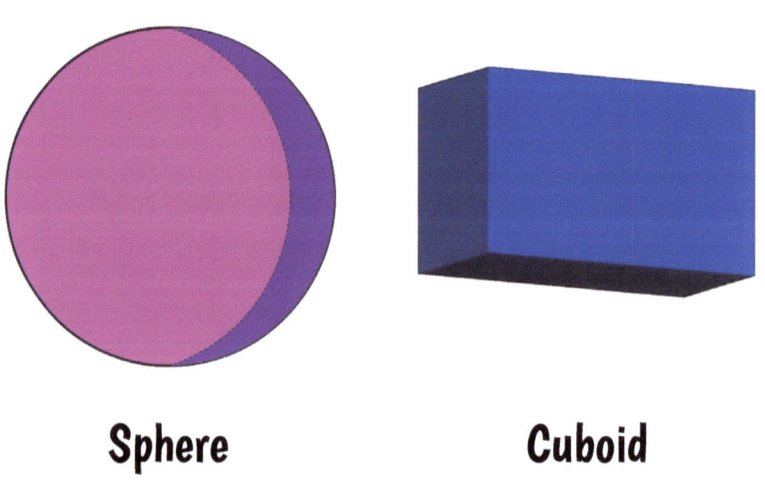

Sphere **Cuboid**

Other Sapo Children's Books you will love...

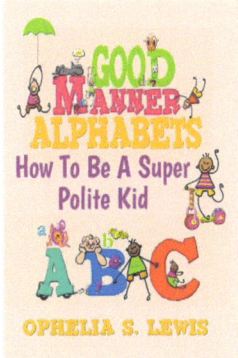

Available everywhere books are sold.

Paperback & eBook

www.villagetalespublishing.com

Connect With Us

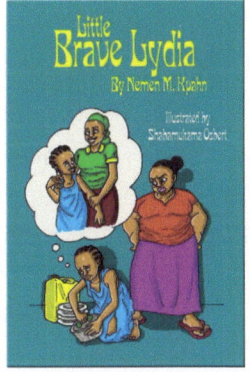 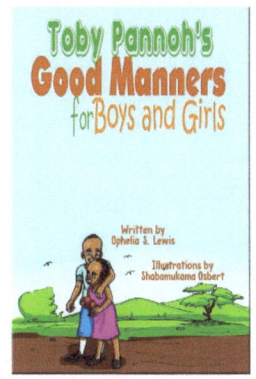 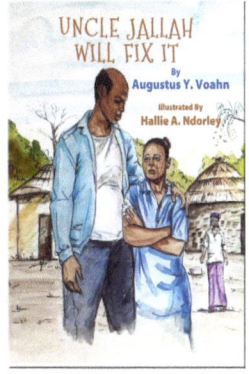

  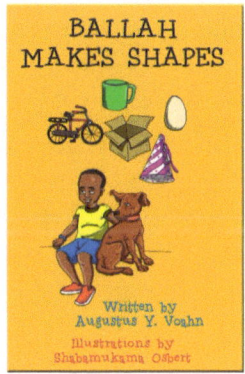

Author, Augustus Y. Voahn

Augustus Y. Voahn was born in Zuolay, Nimba County, in the northeastern region of Liberia. Mr. Voahn worked in many rural communities in Liberia, including Community Development, Child Protection, Women Empowerment and Girls Education. A book lover since childhood, Voahn's favorite subjects in school was Literature and English. His first two books, *Under the Bridge* (2010) and *Swimming At ten* (2013) were published through CODE (Canada Overseas Development Education) program. Mr. Voahn joined Liberian-own publishing firm, Village Tales Publishing in 2015. His first book with VTP, *Uncle Jallah Will Fix It*, was published in 2016. *Ballah Makes Shapes* is his second book.

Mr. Voahn writes for both adult and children. He lives in Monrovia with his three beautiful daughters; Gertrude, Augusta and Valerie, who also love reading and writing as well.

Illustrator, Shabamukama Osbert

Shabamukama Osbert was born on July 7, 1990 in the small village of Mbonwa, Ibanda District, Western Uganda. Since his mother died when he was five-years-old, Osbert was raised by a single father in a big family with eleven other siblings. Art has always been a passion, even during his primary and secondary education. In 2016, he earned his bachelor's degree in industrial and fine art from Makerere University.

Mr. Osbert is a painter, structural designer and an illustrator. He loves art. During his free time, he enjoys photography, travelling, painting and doing illustrations.

He currently lives in Kampala, Uganda. You can connect with Mr. Osbert on Facebook, @Ashabo Osbert.

Glossary

3D
Three-dimensional; shape that has height, width and depth.

Author
A person who writes something.

Circle
A line that curves until its ends meet; like a ring.

Community
A group of people living in the same place.

Cone
A 3D shape with a circular base and a curved surface that comes to a point; like a cookie shaped to hold ice cream.

Cube
A solid 3D shape that has six equal square sides.

Cuboid
A 3D shape with six rectangular faces.

Cylinder
A 3D solid with one long round body and two circular bases.

Decagon
A flat shape with ten angles and ten sides.

Diamond Shape
A square shape placed down, with a corner at the bottom.

Heart Shape
This shape is indented at a double rounded top and pointy at the bottom; a symbolic expression of affection / love.

Heptagon
A Polygon shape with seven angles and seven sides.

Hexagon
A polygon shape with six angles and six sides.

Illustrator
Someone who draws pictures, especially for books.

Mathematics
The science that studies and explains numbers, quantities, measurements, shapes, space, and the relationship between them.

Monrovia
Capital City of Liberia.

Neighbor
A person living near another.

Neighborhood
Group of houses or buildings that are together in an area.

Octagon
A polygon shape with eight angles and eight sides.

Oval
Something having the shape of an egg.

Polygon
A flat shape with three or more straight sides.

Pentagon
A flat shape with five angles and five sides.

Pyramid
A 3D shape with a polygon base and three or more triangles for its sides; structures built especially in ancient Egypt.

Rectangle
A rectangle has two sets of equal opposite sides.

Shape
The form or outline of something.

Sphere
A perfectly round 3D shape similar to a round ball.

Square
A shape with four equal sides.

Star Shape
A shape with five or more points.

Triangle
Something that has three angles (corners) and three sides.

www.ingramcontent.com/pod-product-compliance
Lightning Source LLC
Chambersburg PA
CBHW041755040426
42446CB00001B/46